SERMON OUTLINES
ON THE
CROSS OF
CHRIST

Books by Al Bryant

SERMON OUTLINES
ON THE
CROSS OF CHRIST

compiled by
Al Bryant

kregel
PUBLICATIONS

Grand Rapids, MI 49501

Sermon Outlines on the Cross of Christ © 1993 by Al
Bryant and published by Kregel Publications, a division of
Kregel, Inc., P.O. Box 2607, Grand Rapids, MI 49501. All
rights reserved.

Cover and book design: Alan G. Hartman

Library of Congress Cataloging-in-Publication Data

Sermon outlines on the cross of Christ / compiled by Al
Bryant.

    p.   cm.

    1. Sermons—Outlines, syllabi, etc. I. Bryant, Al, 1926-
BV4223.0435   1993   251'.02—dc20   92-23981
                                                  CIP

ISBN 0-8254-2189-6

        2 3 4 5 Printing/Year 97 96

Printed in the United States of America

CONTENTS

PREFACE

The cross of Christ is the supreme demonstration of God's love for sinful man. In Jesus' death God forthrightly confronts the sin and guilt which offends His holiness and separates us from our Creator. Because of the cross God becomes both the righteous and just Judge, and at the same time, the One who makes forgiveness available and justifies believers. God's condemnation against man has been "canceled," nailed to the cross. The work of the cross is God's means of reconciliation as well as the symbol of our discipleship which becomes a part of the identification between Christ and the believer who is "crucified with Christ."

In brief, this is the criterion used in the selection of the sermon outlines included in this compilation. They cover many phases of the history and meaning of the cross in the Scriptures, as well as the actual event itself.

AL BRYANT

TEXTUAL INDEX

BEHOLD THE MAN

    I.   The Despised man.
"He was despised" (Isa. 53:3).

   II.   The Rejected man.
"Not this Man but Barabbas" (John 18:40).

  III.   The Crucified man.
"By wicked hands have crucified" (Acts 2:23).

  IV.   The Approved man.
"A Man approved of God" (Acts 2:22).

   V.   The Perfect man.
"I find no fault in this Man" (Luke 23:4).

  VI.   The Righteous man.
"This was a righteous Man" (Luke 23:47).

 VII.   The Risen man.
"Whom God hath raised up" (Acts 2:24).

VIII.   The Coming man.
"The Son of Man shall come" (Matt. 16:27).

CHARLES INGLIS

THE BETRAYAL OF CHRIST

And they were exceeding sorrowful, and began every one of them to say unto Him, Lord, is it I? (Matt. 26:22).

    I.   The language of painful surprise.

   II.   The language of conscious innocence.

  III.   The language of self-mistrust.

SELECTED

CHRIST'S PERFECTION

Christ was perfect in all He was, in all He said, in all He did, and in all His life.

I.   There was no rift in the fabric of His character, for He did always the things which were pleasing to His Father (Matt. 3:17).

II. There was no flaw in the devotion of His life, for He knew no sin (2 Cor. 5:21).

III. There was no fault in the consecration of His service, for He finished the work given Him to do (John 17:4).

IV. There was no stain in the texture of His nature, for He was without sin (1 John 3:5).

V.   There was no alloy in the gold of His holiness, for He was the Holy One of God (Mark 1:24).

VI. There was no spot in the sun of His testimony, for He did no sin (1 Peter 2:22).

VII. There was no lack in the obedience of His love, for He was faithful to death (Phil. 2:8).

F. E. MARSH

DEATH OF CHRIST

1. The death of Christ is the *record* of the greatest sin that was ever committed (Acts. 2:23).

2. The *exhibition* of the greatest love ever seen (Rom. 5:8).

3. The *manifestation* of the greatest victory that was ever achieved (Heb. 2:14).

4. The *introduction* of the greatest force ever (1 John 3:16).

5. The *unlocking* of the greatest problem that has ever engaged man's attention (1 Peter 1:11).

6. The *supply* of the greatest incentive ever given (2 Cor. 5:14).

7. The *evidence* of the greatest example we can ever imitate (Eph. 5:2).

F. E. MARSH

CHRIST'S PRAYER IN GETHSEMANE

The characteristics of the prayer of Christ are:

I.   It was a lonely prayer. He withdrew Himself about a stone's cast from His disciples, as He went to prayer (Luke 22:41).

II. It was a humble prayer. In Mark, we are told Christ "knelt," and in Matthew, that He fell upon His face. The attitude of His body is an indication of the posture of His spirit.

III. It was a filial prayer. He does not say here, as He did afterwards, "My God," etc., but "Abba Father." The former reminds of God's dealing in judgment with sin: the latter is the Father making known His will (Mark 14:36).

IV. It was an earnest prayer (Luke 22:44; Heb. 5:7).

V.   It was a repeated prayer. He used "the same words" (Matt. 26:44).

VI. It was a persevering prayer. He prayed three times (Matt. 26:44).

VII. It was a resigned prayer. "Not My will," etc. (Luke 22:42). "My will, not thine, be done," turned Paradise into a desert; and "Thy will, not Mine be done," turned the desert into a Paradise.

VIII. It was an answered prayer. In Luke 22:43, we are told an angel came and strengthened Him.

F. E. MARSH

SEVEN SAYINGS OF CHRIST ON THE CROSS

1. Prayer: "Father forgive" (Luke 23:34).
2. Promise: "With Me in Paradise" (Luke 23:43).
3. Provision: "Woman, behold Thy Son" (John 19:26).
4. Position: "Why hast Thou forsaken Me?" (Matt. 27:46).
5. Pain: "I thirst" (John 19:28).
6. Perfection: "It is finished" (John 19:30).
7. Presentation: "Into Thy hands I commend My Spirit" (Luke 23:46).

CHARLES INGLIS

THE CRIES OF CHRIST

I. The Cry of the Witness.

"Jesus *cried* and said, He that believeth on Me believeth not on Me, but on Him that sent Me" (John 12:44). Faithful in its testimony and full in its promise.

II. The Cry of the Teacher.

"He *cried*, He that hath ears to hear, let him hear" (Luke 8:8). Powerful in utterance and practical in outcome.

III. The Cry of the Life-giver.

"He *cried* with a loud voice, Lazarus, come forth" (John 11:43). Quickening and liberating.

IV. The Cry of the Satisfier.

"Jesus stood and *cried*, saying, If any man thirst let him come unto Me and drink" (John 8:37). Sure, lasting, refreshing and free.

V. The Cry of the Rebuker.

"Then *cried* Jesus in the Temple as He taught, saying, ye both know Me," etc. (John 7:28). Searching and mouth-stopping.

VI. The Cry of the Surrenderer.

"Jesus *crying* with a loud voice, said, Father into Thy hands," etc. (Luke 23:46, R.V., M.). Patient and passive.

VII. The Cry of the Sufferer.

"Jesus *cried* with a loud voice saying, My God! why hast Thou forsaken Me?" (Matt. 27:46). Cry of Cries.

F. E. MARSH

THE DEATH OF CHRIST

The pith and power of the gospel are the death and resurrection of Christ. The former is its pith, and the latter is its power. The death of Christ is:

I. **Real as to Its Occurrence.**
"Christ that *died*" (Rom. 8:34). "Christ *died*" (Rom. 14:15; 1 Cor. 8:11). Towering over the wrecks of time, there is one fact that shines out in unmistakable reality, and that is, the death of Christ.

II. **Substitutionary in Its Character.**
"Christ *died* for the ungodly," "Christ *died* for us" (Rom. 5:6-8). Christ was acting on our behalf that He might protect us from the consequence of sin in dying in our stead.

III. **Definite in Its Work.**
"He *died* unto sin once" (Rom. 6:10). "Christ *died* for our sins" (1 Cor. 15:3). His death had distinct relation to our sin. He died to bear away our *sins*, and to be judged for our *sin*.

IV. **Freeing in Its Aim.**
"He *died* for all, that they which live should not henceforth live unto themselves, but unto Him who *died* for them and rose again" (2 Cor. 5:15). In the death of Christ we have the magnet which draws us from self to Himself.

V. **Practical in Its Purpose.**
"To this end Christ both *died*, and rose, and revived, that He might be Lord both of the dead and living" (Rom. 14:9). He died that He might gain us, and now we are His absolute property.

VI. **Assurance of Future Glory.**
"Who *died* for us, that, whether we wake or sleep, we should live together with Him" (1 Thess. 5:10). The blood-red mark of Christ's cross is stamped on every certificate of heaven.

VII. **Guarantee That Our Loved Ones, Who Have Fallen Asleep, Shall Be with Us in Christ's Coming Glory.**
"If we believe that Jesus *died* and rose again, even so them also which sleep in Jesus will God bring with Him" (1 Thess. 4:14). There is one ray that shall make the golden glory of Christ's splendor bear a rosy tint, and that is the blood-red light of Calvary.

F. E. MARSH

SUBSTITUTION OF CHRIST

The Apostle Paul, in writing to the Church at Corinth, said, "I will very gladly spend and be spent for you" (2 Cor. 12:15). The preposition "huper," translated "for," is the one Paul uses, and is applied to Christ as the One who was not only willing, but who did "spend" and was "spent out" (2 Cor. 12:15, R.V., M.), in acting on our behalf. The meaning of the word is bending over to protect, as a mother bird will cover her young at the sacrifice of her own life; or service rendered on behalf of another, thus acting in his stead, as when the priest offered "sacrifices *for* sins" on behalf of another (Heb. 5:1). The following will illustrate how faithfully and fully Christ acted on behalf of those who believe in Him. The preposition *"huper"* occurs in each case, and is rendered *"for."*

1. Christ as Giver. "Given for you" (Luke 22:19; 1 Cor. 11:24).

2. Christ as Atoner. "Shed for you" (Luke 22:20).

3. Christ as the Bread. "Bread . . . for the life of the world" (John 6:51).

4. Christ as the Good Shepherd. "Good Shepherd giveth His life for the sheep" (John 10:11).

5. Christ as the Volunteer. "I lay down My life for the sheep" (John 10:15).

6. Christ as the Provision for ungodly ones and sinners. "Christ died for the ungodly" (Rom. 5:6); "Christ died for us" (Rom. 5:8).

7. Christ as the Passover. "Christ our Passover, sacrificed for us" (1 Cor. 5:7).

8. Christ as the Fulfiller of Scripture. "Christ died for our sins according to the Scriptures" (1 Cor. 15:3).

9. Christ as the Sin-bearer. "He hath made Him to be sin for us" (2 Cor. 5:21).

10. Christ as the Deliverer. "Gave Himself for our sins, that He might deliver" (Gal. 1:4).

11. Christ as the Substitute. "Gave Himself for me" (Gal. 2:20).

12. Christ as the Curse-bearer. "Made a curse for us" (Gal. 3:13).

13. Christ as the Burnt-offering. "Himself for us, an offering and a sacrifice to God for a sweet-smelling savor" (Eph. 5:2).

14. Christ as the Lover. "Loved . . . . gave Himself for it" (Eph. 5:25).

15. Christ as the Savior. "Salvation through our Lord Jesus Christ, who died for us" (1 Thess. 5:10, R.V.).

16. Christ as the Ransom. "A Ransom for all" (1 Tim. 2:6).

17. Christ as the Redeemer. "Gave Himself for us, that He might redeem us," etc. (Titus 2:14).

18. Christ as the Kinsman. "Taste death for every man" (Heb. 2:9).

19. Christ as the Sacrifice. "Sacrifice for sins" (Heb. 10:12).

20. Christ as the Sufferer. "Suffered for us" (1 Peter 2:21).

21. Christ as the Reconciler. "Just for the unjust, that He might bring us to God" (1 Peter 3:18).

22. Christ as the Example. "Christ hath suffered for us . . . . likewise," etc. (1 Peter 4:1).

23. Christ as the Inspirer. "He laid down His life for us, and we ought," etc. (1 John 3:16).

We have thus given in detail the principal Scriptures that speak of Christ's vicarious action, as it is of essential importance to be clear upon the main fact, for to be wrong here is to be wrong at every point.

F. E. MARSH

SACRIFICE OF CHRIST

I. Necessary Sacrifice.
"What the law could not do, in that it was weak, through the flesh, God sending His own Son in the likeness of sinful flesh, and by a *sacrifice* for sin (margin), condemned sin in the flesh" (Rom. 8:3).

II. Offered Sacrifice.
"Who needeth not daily to offer up *sacrifice*. . . . He offered up Himself" (Heb. 7:27).

III. Removing Sacrifice.
"Put away sin by the *sacrifice* of Himself"(Heb. 9:26).

IV. Perfect Sacrifice.
"Offered one *sacrifice* for sins forever" (Heb. 10:12).

V. Accepted Sacrifice.
"Christ. . . . hath given Himself for us, an offering and a *sacrifice* to God for a sweet smelling savor"(Eph. 5:2).

VI. Substitutionary Sacrifice.
"Christ, our Passover, is *sacrificed* for us" (1 Cor. 5:7).

VII. Remembered Sacrifice.
"Gather My saints together unto Me, those that have made a covenant with Me by *sacrifice*" (Psalm 50:5).

F. E. Marsh

RESURRECTION OF CHRIST

The resurrection of Christ is the *heart* of Christianity, which makes it pulsate with the life of God; it is the *keystone* to the arch of truth, which holds all the faith of the Gospel together; it is the *foundation* of the church; it is the *mainspring* of Christian activity; it is the *lever* of power which shall move the world; and it is the *link* that unites all believers.

The death of Christ tells us of the *love* of *God*, and the resurrection of Christ tells us of the *power* of *God*, and of the following seven facts:

1. That God is satisfied and glorified (Rom. 8:33,34).

2. That our sins are gone (Eph. 1:7).

3. That we are accepted in Christ (Eph. 1:6).

4. That we are united to Christ (Col. 2:12; 3:1).

5. That every foe is vanquished (Col. 2:15).

6. That we shall forever live with Him (John 14:19).

7. That the Spirit is given to the believer (John 7:39).

Further, the resurrection of Christ was announced in the Scriptures. The death, burial, and resurrection of Christ were "according to the Scriptures." Mainly the Old Testament is meant when the New Testament speaks of "the Scriptures." Where, in the Old Testament, is the resurrection of Christ mentioned? Peter, on the Day of Pentecost, by the Holy Spirit, says in the "sixteenth Psalm" (Psalm 16:8-11; Acts 2:24-32); and Paul at Antioch says in the "second Psalm" (Psalm 2:7; Acts 13:32-37). The God-breathed Scriptures (2 Tim. 3:16) were the basis and the authority of the utterance of the apostles, therefore they had an authority above all question, for "where the word of a king is, there is power" (Eccl. 8:4); and the hearers who received their message had a solid rock upon which to rest, which could never be moved (1 Cor. 15:1-4).

F. E. MARSH

DEATH OF CHRIST AND THE CROSS

The cross of Calvary was ever casting its terrible shadow across the path of Christ. It is interesting and instructive to mark Christ's repeated reference to His death. The death of Christ is:

1. The testimony to man's sin (Acts 2:23).
2. The triumph of God's grace (Heb. 2:9).
3. The trysting place where God and the sinner can meet (1 Tim. 2:5,6).
4. The title to eternal life (John 12:24).
5. The temple for refuge (Heb. 9:12-14).
6. The teacher for instruction (Titus 2:11,12).
7. The tether for binding (Gal. 2:20).

F. E. MARSH

FORGOTTEN CROSS

Rev. W. H. Armstrong, in speaking at a Wesleyan Conference in England of the influence of the early Methodist preachers and those of today, said: "He ventured to think the reason for this was, that in emphasizing the social implications of the Christian Gospel they had forgotten the Cross, which was the only effective dynamic of social service." The dynamic of the Cross is seen if we, having recognized its objective work (1 Cor. 15:3,4), ponder its subjective influence.

1. The Cross is the death of sin (Rom. 6:10,11).
2. The slayer of self (Gal. 2:20).
3. The separator from the world (Gal. 6:14).
4. The begetter of love to others (1 John 3:16).
5. The soul of holiness (Heb. 13:12, 20,21).
6. The incentive to sacrifice (Matt. 20:26-28).
7. The main-spring of service (2 Cor. 5:14).
8. The music of worship (Rev. 5:9,10).
9. The hope of the future (1 Thess. 4:13,14).

F. E. MARSH

FOURTEEN APPEARINGS OF CHRIST AFTER HIS RESURRECTION

There are no less than *fourteen* recorded appearings of Christ before Paul wrote to the Church of Corinth, and fifteen if we include Christ's manifestation to John in the Isle of Patmos. The fourteen appearings are as follows:

1. To Mary Magdalene (John 20:14; Mark 16:9).

2. To the other women (Matt. 28:9).

3. To Peter (1 Cor. 15:5; Luke 24:34).

4. To the two disciples on their way to Emmaus (Mark 16:12,13; Luke 24:13-32).

5. The day He appeared to the disciples, in the absence of Thomas (John 20:19-24).

6. To the disciples when Thomas was present (John 20:24-29).

7. To Galilee, at the sea of Tiberias, to Peter, John, Thomas, James, Nathanael, and two others (John 21:1-14).

8. To the disciples on a mount in Galilee (Matt. 28:16).

9. To more than five hundred brethren at once (1 Cor. 15:6).

10. To James the apostle (1 Cor. 15:7).

11. To all the apostles assembled together (1 Cor. 15:7).

12. To all the apostles at His ascension (Luke 24:50,51; Acts 1:9,10).

13. To Stephen, when he was being stoned to death (Acts 7:56).

14. To Paul (1 Cor. 15:8; Acts 9:3-5; 22:6-10).

Such a mass of evidence attesting any given fact would be accepted as proof positive as to its validity in any court of justice.

F. E. MARSH

"And the pleasure of the Lord shall prosper in His hand" (Isa. 53:10).

In no part of the prophetic writings are the humiliation and sufferings of Christ detailed with such affecting minuteness as in this chapter, and inveterate indeed must have been the blindness and unbelief of the Jews, not to perceive and admit the force of such overwhelming evidence. The same prophecy, however, foretold that the report would not be believed, and that when the Savior should appear He would be rejected and despised of men. Nevertheless He shall see His seed, He shall prolong His days, and the pleasure of the Lord shall prosper in His hand.

I.   A Few Explanatory Remarks on the Terms of the Text.

A.   By "the pleasure of the Lord" we are to understand, *His purposes concerning the cause of Christ*. It was an important part of His good pleasure, that sinners should be redeemed by the blood of Christ, and this He delighted to accomplish (Ps. 40:6-8). But this part of the will of God is supposed in the text to be already effected, and that another part is immediately to follow, relating to the progress of Christ's kingdom.

B.   The success of Christ's undertaking, in the universal spread of the gospel, is called *the pleasure of the Lord*, because it is an object of His eternal purpose, and the end He had in view in the creation of the world (Col. 1:16). It is true indeed, the accomplishment of God's design is said to be His pleasure, even when it relates to the punishment of His enemies; for "He will do His pleasure on Babylon, and His arm shall be on the Chaldeans"; but that in which He takes peculiar delight is the enlargement of Christ's kingdom. God takes pleasure in all His works, but more in the work of redemption than any other, and more still in rewarding the obedience and sufferings of His well-beloved Son, than in putting Him to grief (John 10:17; Phil. 2:9).

C.   The great work of subduing the world is here placed *in the hand of Christ*. The work of redeeming sinners was committed to Him, and He succeeded in that; and now the work of subduing the nations to the obedience of faith is put into His hand. He is head over all things to the church, and all shall be made subservient to His will. All power in heaven and earth is given unto Him, and

He is sending forth His armies, that He may rule in the midst of His enemies, and triumph over all the earth (Pss. 45:3,4; 110:1-3).

D. It is here foretold that the work of Christ *shall certainly succeed*, and the pleasure of the Lord "shall prosper in His hand." If placed in other hands it would have failed, but with Him it must prosper. Adam was constituted the federal head of his posterity, but he failed in the undertaking, and all were ruined. Moses was charged with the redemption of Israel, but he failed of bringing them into the promised land; and as to the eternal salvation of any of them, it was effected only by the death of Christ, and not by the law of Moses. All others have failed and been discouraged, but He shall set judgment in the earth, and the isles shall wait for His law. Thousands among the Jews, and tens of thousands among the Gentiles, have submitted to His authority; and He shall still go on and prosper, till the whole earth be filled with His glory.

II. The Reasons Why the Pleasure of the Lord Should Prosper in the Hand of Christ.

Two things are generally necessary to the success of any great undertaking; one is, personal fitness or qualification, and the other, the means of accomplishing the design.

A. Christ possesses, in an eminent degree, *the qualifications* necessary to the work He has undertaken. Great and unconquerable zeal is required, where the work is arduous and attended with great difficulty, and nothing can be done without it. If a man, from mere worldly motives, engages in the work of the ministry, he will not be likely to succeed; his efforts and his zeal are totally inadequate to so important an undertaking. But Christ's heart was wholly set upon what He undertook, and His zeal shall bring it to pass (Isa. 63:4). Wisdom also is required. A good intention, accompanied with ardent exertions, is not sufficient; wisdom and understanding are necessary to conduct things to a proper issue; and these qualifications are possessed in an eminent degree by the blessed Savior (Isa. 3:13). Faithfulness also to His engagements was eminently verified in Him (Isa. 11:5; Heb. 3:2).

B. Christ possesses *all the necessary means* for carrying on His own cause in the world. In consequence of His death the Holy Spirit is given, to convince the world of sin, and to give success to a preached gospel. Christ is able also to save to the uttermost them that come unto God by Him, and that in consequence of His intercession before the throne. He can keep us from falling, and present us faultless before the presence of His glory with exceeding joy. All the arrangements of providence are in His hands; the fate of kingdoms and of empires, and whatever is necessary to the prosperity of His own most righteous cause, are entirely at His command.

Let us reflect,

1.   That as God has entrusted His own glory in the hands of Christ, it becomes us to commit our all to Him, that He may save us in the great day.
2.   That those who labor with Christ in His cause have reason to take encouragement, for it is in His hands, and must finally prevail.

CONDENSED FROM CHARLES SIMEON

THE THREE CROSSES AT CALVARY

"And when they were come to the place which is called Calvary," etc. *(Luke 23:33).*

I.   The Motive of the Rulers in Crucifying Christ Between Two Malefactors.

To make His death seem as odious as possible; to brand Him as a great criminal.

II.   The Unforeseen Result of Their Malice.

The cross became a tribunal. The scene at the Day of Judgment was foreshadowed; the Judge in the center; on one side a penitent; on the other an impenitent sinner. A malefactor became a witness to Christ's mighty, redeeming love.

Lessons:

1.   The same cross attracts and repels.
2.   The most hopeless may obtain mercy.
3.   You may be near the means of salvation, but be lost.

SELECTED

THE SUFFERINGS OF CHRIST

"Yet it pleased the Lord to bruise Him," etc. (Isa. 53:10,11).

Of all the prophetic writings, none contain more clear and correct predictions of Christ, than those of Isaiah; and of all Isaiah's writings, none describe the Messiah more accurately, both in His suffering and exalted state, than this chapter. That the prophet here speaks of our Lord Jesus Christ is evident from the words of the Holy Spirit in the New Testament. He applies Isaiah 53:4 to our Lord (Matt. 8:16,17); He "healed all who were sick, that it might be fulfilled which was spoken by Esaias the prophet, saying, Himself took our infirmities, and bare our sicknesses." He applies Isaiah 53:5 to Him (1 Peter 2:24), "Who His own self bare our sins in His own body on the tree, that we being dead unto sin, should live unto righteousness; by whose stripes ye were healed." He applies Isaiah 53:7,8 to Him (Acts 8:32-35), "The place of the Scriptures which He read, was this, He was led as a sheep to the slaughter; and like a lamb dumb before His shearers, so opened He not His mouth. In His humiliation His judgment was taken from the earth. And the eunuch answered Philip, and said, I pray thee of whom speaketh the prophet this; of himself, or of some other man? Then Philip opened his mouth, and began at the same Scripture, and preached unto him Jesus." This example teaches us that we also may, and indeed should, preach Jesus from the words now before us. For here we find a most interesting description of His character, His sufferings, and the happy effects of His sufferings. We are led to observe—

I. His Character. He was God's righteous Servant, of whom God had before spoken by this prophet (Isa. 52:1).

    A. *He was God's Servant* who glorified God by obeying Him (John 17:4). He served God *fully*: His obedience was complete (Phil. 2:8). "Being," etc. He served God *cheerfully*; without intermission (John 8:29). He served God *unweariedly*; till the work assigned Him was done. He labored on and ceased not, till He was enabled to say, "I have glorified Thee on earth, I have finished the work Thou gavest Me to do."

    B. *He was God's righteous Servant*: being unblamable in all His deportment, and never justly chargeable with sin. This appears—From the testimony of His *friends*; of Paul (2 Cor. 21), "who made," etc.; of Peter (1 Peter 2:22), "Who did," etc.; and of

John (1 John 3:5). "In Him was no sin." And from the testimony of His *enemies*. This was given by Judas, who betrayed Him (Matt. 27:3,4); by Pilate, who condemned Him to death (Matt. 27:24); and by the centurion, whose soldiers crucified Christ, "Certainly," says he, "this was a righteous man; truly this man was the Son of God" (Luke 22:47; Mark 15:39).

C. As God's righteous Servant, *He became a perfect example*, and an *acceptable mediator*. A *perfect example* to all His followers, of piety toward God; love to mankind; and personal purity (Phil. 2:5; 1 John 2:6). And an *acceptable mediator*. For it was requisite that our High Priest should be harmless (Heb. 7:26). and that our Advocate should be righteous (1 John 2:1). "This was requisite, that God's righteousness might be declared in our salvation" (Rom. 3:25,26). Hence let us observe—

II. His Sufferings. "It pleased the Lord to bruise Him," etc. Here we learn,

A. *The extent of His sufferings*. He suffered,

In His body. He was bruised by cruel blows (Matt. 27:30); He was wounded by the thorns, nails, and spear (v. 5); He endured stripes by scourging (v. 5); compare John 19:1, "Then Pilate took Jesus and scourged Him."

In His soul. He was put to grief by the sins of mankind; the cruelty of His avowed enemies (see Ps. 22:14-16); and the treachery of His professing friends; of Judas, who betrayed Him; of Peter, who denied Him; and the other disciples who forsook Him (Matt. 26:56; Zech. 13:6). He was also put to grief by diabolical suggestions (Luke 22:53; Heb. 2:18); and by the suspension of divine comfort (Matt. 36:38, and 37:46). We here learn,

B. *The singularity of His sufferings*. These being unlike those of others, He might properly adopt Jeremiah's language in another case (Lam. 1:12) for His sufferings were *unmerited*. He was perfectly righteous; and the only one who ever suffered without being sinful in nature or practice. His sufferings were *inflicted by God*; not merely by wicked men. God laid them on Him (v. 6). God bruised Him; put Him to grief; and made His soul an offering for sin. Wicked men indeed were the instruments of His sufferings; but God gave Him up to death (Acts 2:23; Rom. 8:12). His sufferings were *pleasing to God*. It pleased God to bruise Him. He did not afflict Christ reluctantly, as He does His other children (Lam. 3:22,23). And yet our Lord *concurred* in His sufferings. His soul was made an offering for sin, readily, without hesitation; He poured out His soul unto death, as His own voluntary act and deed (v. 12); He laid down His life freely, not by compulsion (John 10:15, 18; Mark 10:45). Hence let us observe,

C. *The general nature of His sufferings*. They were evidently vicarious; or sufferings endured by Him as a substitute for others.

He became an *offering* for the *sin* of others, in their stead (2 Cor. 5:21; 1 Peter 3:18). He bore the iniquities of *others*. "He shall bear their iniquities," or the punishment due to their iniquities, by just desert; as the loss of divine comfort, the curse and death (Gal. 3:13,14), "Christ hath," etc. His sufferings were a *"travail"*; this implies that they were pains endured by Him, for the benefit of others: to make them heirs of glory (Heb. 2:10); to heal them (Isa. 53:5); and bring them to God (1 Peter 3:18). This leads us to consider,

III. The Happy Effects of His Sufferings. In consequence thereof—

A. *He shall prolong His days*. By rising from death to immortal life (Rev. 1:13). This was effected by Himself; according to His own declarations (John 2:19, and 10:13). And it was the reward of His obedience unto death (Isa. 53:12; Phil. 2:8-11).

B. *He shall justify many by His knowledge*. "By His knowledge," etc. This implies that through or by the knowledge of Him, many will obtain justification. By justification is meant the forgiveness of sins. Compare Acts 13:33 and 39. The knowledge of Christ includes a just view of Him as the only acceptable mediator between God and men (John 14:6; 1 Tim. 2:5); a cordial approbation of Him (1 Cor. 2:2); and affiance in Him (Ps. 9:10). All who thus know Him, are justified through and by Him (Rom. 5:1; Acts 13:39; John 14:6; 1 Tim. 2:5).

C. *He shall see His seed*: or His posterity, the fruit of His travail. This shall be a *numerous* seed (Heb. 2:10; Pss. 2:8 and 110:3). And a *hopeful* seed; a general blessing (Matt. 5:13,14); and finally happy (Isa. 35:10). He shall *see* His seed: see them *flocking to Him* for salvation (Isa. 60:8); see them *saved by Him* on earth (Isa. 8:18); and *glorified with Him* in heaven (Rev. 3:21 and 17:14).

D. *The pleasure of the Lord shall prosper in His hand*. The pleasure of the Lord is His church; the object of His delight (Isa. 63:4; Ps. 147:11). This is in Christ's hand; under His government and care (Deut. 33:3; John 10:27,28). It shall prosper there; be kept uninjured (Matt. 16:18) and extend universally (Dan. 2:44).

E. *He shall see of the travail of His soul, and shall be satisfied.* He shall witness the blessings enjoyed by His redeemed servants: their interest in God's favor; their spiritual life, comfort, and honor (Rev. 7:15-17). And seeing this He will be well pleased that He has endured the curse, death, grief, and shame for them (Ps. 35:27; Zeph. 3:17). From Christ's sufferings,

1. *Learn your obligations to cultivate a spirit of contrition*, or godly sorrow, on account of sin. Because your sins occasioned His sufferings at first (Zech. 12:10). And they have since crucified Him afresh (Heb. 6:6; Ps. 38:18).

2. *Your encouragement, if penitent, to hope for salvation.* For Christ was *given* for your benefit (Rom. 8:32), and is *exalted* for your benefit (Ps. 68:18).

3. *God's claims on you as the subjects of redeeming grace.* On your *services* (1 Cor. 6:19,20; Rom. 12:1; Ps. 116:1,2; Rev. 1:5,6). "Unto Him that loved us."

CONDENSED FROM CHARLES SIMEON

THE PRIESTLY INTERCESSION OF CHRIST

I. The Place:
   A. The Father's throne in heaven—Hebrews 9:1-8, 11,12, 24; Romans 8:34.

II. For Whom:
   A. Christians only—Hebrews 9:24; 7:24,25; John 17:9.

III. The Basis of the Plea:
   A. The blood—Hebrews 9:12.
   B. The finished work—John 17:1-8.

IV. The Plea:
   A. For grace and glory—John 17:9-26.

V. The Special Purposes of the Plea:
   A. To justify—Romans 4:25.
   B. To give and maintain life—Romans 5:10; Hebrews 9:24; Romans 8:34; 1 John 2:1; Hebrews 7:24,25.
   C. To provide cleansing—1 John 2:1, with 1 John 1:9.
   D. To give grace and help—Hebrews 4:15,16.
   E. To answer prayer—John 16:23-26.
   F. To secure victory—Hebrews 2:17,18.

HENRY W. FROST

"My soul is exceeding sorrowful, even unto death" (Matt. 26:38).

The sufferings of Christ are one of the great mysteries of godliness. We know but little, and cannot fully comprehend what they mean, but it would be happy for us if we were better acquainted with their meaning. It was Paul's prayer, that he might know the fellowship of Christ's sufferings, made conformable unto His death.

The manner in which our Lord spent the last night, the night before His suffering, is highly impressive. He went with His disciples to the house of a friend in Jerusalem; and when evening was come, they entered an upper room to eat the passover. After this the supper of the Lord was instituted. Judas left the room, and had an interview with the Jews, according to a previous appointment. While he was gone, Jesus delivered His farewell discourse to His disciples, which is given in John 14-17. At the close of this affecting address, Jesus offered up His intercessory prayer, in the hearing of His disciples. Taking with Him His close friends, Peter, James, and John, He entered into the garden of Gethsemane; and there He began to be "very heavy, and sore amazed." The disciples beheld His agony, and heard the distressing words recorded in our text. Let us,

I. Consider the fact: "His Soul Was Exceeding Sorrowful."

It was so indeed, and to such a degree as exceeded all His former sufferings. Christ's own testimony is sufficient to prove this: He never affected grief, nor magnified His sufferings. Great sorrows generally precede loud complaints, and are like deep waters, which run the stillest. It was thus with Job, and also with Jesus. He made no great complaint—a few words to His friends, and a few to His heavenly Father, are all that dropped from His lips (Isa. 53:7; 1 Peter 2:23).

Nearly all the evangelists have given an account of His sufferings in the garden, which they describe in various affecting forms of speech. Mark tells us that He began to be "sore amazed" (14:33). Luke, that He was "in an agony, sweating as it were great drops of blood, falling to the ground." Matthew tells us that He was "exceeding sorrowful even unto death." What a scene was this?

Sorrow is the fruit of sin; but here was no sin, though He was treated as if He had been the chief of sinners, yea the only sinner in the world—as if divine vengeance had forgotten to run in its usual channels, it concentrated all in Him. Blessed Savior! Considering the infinite dignity of His person, and how much He was the object of the Father's delight; the scene is full of awful grandeur, and such as was never before exhibited.

II. Endeavor to Account for It.

If Christ died merely as a martyr, as some have pretended, the overwhelming nature of His sufferings could not be accounted for. On this scheme, He would appear very inferior to many of His followers, who have suffered death for His sake with heroic fortitude. Some indeed who deny the deity and atonement of Christ, have endeavored to remove the difficulty by allowing that Christ is not only a mere man, but a very imperfect one, and bring this transaction in the garden as an instance of His timidity. Thus has the Savior of the world been degraded by His followers, and betrayed by His professed friends. Let us dread dishonoring the Savior, by attempting to account for His agony in such a way as this.

In general, we may observe, it was now that the Father *withdrew Himself* from His beloved Son: and He cried out: "My God! My God! why hast Thou forsaken Me!"

It was now also that He poured out *His wrath* to the uttermost upon Him. As He had become the sinner's Surety, He must feel the weight of that curse which the sinner had deserved; and who knows the power of that anger! Who can estimate the tremendous evil of sin? Even Jesus Himself was "sore amazed."

Now it was the *prince of this world* came to make his last desperate attack upon Him: this was the hour and the power of darkness. The enemy had before tried what he could do by temptation; and now he will try what the most awful terrors may accomplish (John 14:30). All these things meeting together, His soul became "exceeding sorrowful, even unto death." More particularly—

A. *The greatness of His mind* rendered Him more susceptible of grief than we can possibly experience or imagine. As man, His intimate union with the divine nature, gave an enlargement to His powers beyond our highest conceptions. It was no small part of Job's affliction that he was to be set at naught by persons so inferior to himself, and toward whom it would have been an act of condescension to have noticed them in any other circumstances.

B. His *infinite purity* freed Him from all partiality. He therefore saw things as they were, and had a full view of the infinite evil of sin, as it affected the righteous government of God; and this would render Him susceptible of the greatness of His displeasure against it. It is this which gives an edge to punishment: if God's displeasure against sin had been arbitrary, or severe beyond measure, even hell itself would be tolerable, and Christ would not have felt what He did. We can bear contempt or suffering much better when we know they are undeserved, than when it is otherwise. All that Christ felt, He knew to be the just desert of sin; and this it was that gave poignancy to His sufferings.

C. His *love to the Father* was such that it must necessarily have affected Him in an unknown degree, to be forsaken and put to grief by Him (Isa. 53:10). Frowns may be endured, but not those of a friend: oh why hast *"Thou* forsaken Me!"

D. The love He bore *to the souls of men*, made their conduct toward Him exceeding grievous. Had it been an enemy that should crucify and put Him to open shame, He could have borne it: but He was wounded in the house of His friends, He was put to death by those whose life He came to seek. When Satan came against Him, it did not grieve Him, but raised His abhorrence: but the prospect of suffering by the hands of men, filled Him with bitterness of soul (Heb. 5:7).

III. Application.

A. What a motive is here for *gratitude*, when we consider the results of this dismal hour. From hence it is that the curse is removed, and that the sorrows of the believer have nothing penal in them. Since He has drunk the bitter cup, there is nothing left for us: the means is now prepared for turning our sorrows into endless joys, and our tears into rivers of delight (John 16:20; 2 Cor. 4:17).

B. What a motive for *repentance*, to think of the sorrows which He endured. See what sin has done!

C. Let the example of the suffering Savior teach us *sympathy* toward the afflicted. He bore our sorrows, and carried our griefs: in all our afflictions He Himself was afflicted. Let us learn to bear each other's burdens, and so fulfill the law of Christ (Isa. 63:9; 53:4; Gal. 6:2).

D. Let us also learn *patience* from His example, and consider Him who endured the cross for us, lest we be weary and faint in our minds (Heb. 12:2,3; 1 Peter 2:21-23).

E. From His sufferings we may learn what will be the portion of the finally *impenitent*, who reject His salvation. Their sorrows will be insupportable, and unavailing (Matt. 13:42).   —SIMEON

SIMON OF CYRENE

"And as they came out, they found a man of Cyrene, Simon by name: him they compelled to bear the cross" (Matt. 27:32).

The day of Christ's death, and Easter, or the day of His resurrection, may be easily and correctly ascertained. These events being connected with the great annual festival of the Jewish passover, remove all doubt and difficulty in the matter. It is very different as to the period of Christ's birth, although it is certain it was not on our 25th of December, as kept. But whether in September or October, cannot be decided. The subject of which this day reminds us, is of the greatest possible moment. It is the basis of the whole superstructure of our religion. It is the great center of Christianity. Without it, we have no redemption; for we have no redemption except in His blood, even the forgiveness of sins. This theme should be the leading one in our thoughts and contemplations. It is ever important, and ever interesting. We can consider only some one point within the limits of a discourse. First,

I.   Let Us Contemplate the Condition of the Savior
   A.   Jesus had been condemned to die.
        The history of this mock trial is familiar to all. Innocence had been associated with all that was vile. The Prince of Peace had been falsely accused of sedition; and the devotional Jesus had been treated as a blasphemer; and He, whose life had been expended in miracles of mercy, was declared to be the common enemy of man, and not worthy to live.
   B.   He had been condemned to die by crucifixion.
        This was a Roman punishment, and was associated with all that was shameful and excruciating. None but the very basest were ever put to death in this way. Beheading was the common mode of Roman punishment. In this, then, Christ was reduced to the level of the vilest Roman slave; and thus it was intended that perpetual infamy should be connected with His name. It was a cruel and excruciating death which could last for days. It is said that Andrew lived two days upon the cross. Now, only think of the muscles torn by nails driven through the most tender parts of the hands and feet. Then of the succeeding inflammation and burning fever, scorching up all the moisture of the body, until delirium and death ensued. Now, this was the death to which Christ was adjudged.

C. He was now on the way to crucifixion.

As such, it was common for the transverse beam, or cross, to be laid upon the shoulders of the criminal, so that the spectators might consider the criminal as the sole cause of his infamy and death. However this might apply generally, it was utterly inappropriate on this occasion. Even Pilate had found no fault in Jesus; and had attested His innocence by washing his hands before all the people. On His sacred shoulders, however, they had laid the cross; and it is obvious, He had borne it for some distance, when it became evident He could sustain it no longer. Nature was exhausted, and He fainted beneath the load. Doubtless, His enemies feared He might die before they reached Golgotha, and that they might be deprived of the horrid scene for which they so maliciously thirsted. Need you wonder that Jesus fainted? Just take a retrospect of the twelve preceding hours.

Go back to the room where Jesus was sitting with His disciples, around the sacramental board. Follow Him into the garden of Gethsemane—think of His unutterable agony there. See Him prostrate on the ground, etc. Then see Him rudely dragged to the hall of the high-priest, where He is buffeted, and smitten, and mocked. Then, see Him led to Pilate, from thence to Herod, and back again to Pilate, overpowered by the clamors of the people. See Pilate giving Him up to be crucified. Behold what succeeded (27:27). And after this train of sorrows both of soul and body, do you wonder that He could sustain the cross no further? Now, this leads us,

II. To Consider the Circumstances Stated Respecting Simon.

Simon was a native of Cyrene, a chief city of North Africa. Most likely He was a Jewish proselyte, and had come to the annual festival at Jerusalem. It appears that accidentally He met the cavalcade ascending the hill of Calvary; and, at once they seize him, and compel him to bear the cross of Jesus. But why did they *compel* him to bear the cross? Because, none could do so without being branded with ignominy; and the lowest soldier would have felt himself irreparably degraded by it. The Romans dared not seize a Jew and even Simon could not have been bribed to the task; seeing, however, from his color, that he belonged to the race doomed to be the servants of servants, they seized him; and only by the power of the glittering spears was this African forced into this degrading service. Now, let us consider,

III. What Are the Instructions Suggested by the Whole?

A. We see in the death of Jesus the great antitype of the ancient sacrifices.

No sacrifice so completely pointed to the death of Christ as the passover. The victim—its being roasted with fire; its being eaten with bitter herbs, etc., all pointed to Christ, etc. So also the scapegoat, on the great day of expiation, was led into the wilderness by the hand of any man they met with; and that it was generally a foreigner. So here Jesus, when going forth to bear the sins of the world, had His cross borne by Simon, the Cyrene.

B. We see Providence overruling events, so as to secure the divine glory.

It was necessary that Christ should have aid. Here a bearer of the cross is provided. Besides, it seems clear that it was the means of Simon's conversion. His office brought him into direct contact with Jesus, and the miracles accompanying the crucifixion. He saw, and heard, and felt, as the centurion did, who exclaimed, "Truly this was the Son of God." His sons, Alexander and Rufus, are often mentioned with Christian honor. How diversified are the ways of Providence! "God moves in a mysterious way," etc.

C. Every Christian must be a cross-bearer, and have fellowship with the sufferings of Christ.

"If any man will be My disciple," etc. "If ye suffer with Him," etc. See Hebrews 19:12,13.

"Shall Simon bear the cross alone,
And all the rest go free?
No! Christ has a cross for every one,
He has a cross for me."

D. Let the sinner learn the only way of salvation.

Christ has died for our sins, etc. "Whosoever believeth in Him," etc. We have all we need in Him. Ease from His toil. Health from His wounds. Honor from His shame. Life from His death; and salvation from Him who was made a curse for us, etc.

JABEZ BURNS

CHRIST'S LAMENTATION ON THE CROSS

"My God, My God, why hast Thou forsaken Me?" (Matt. 27:46).

There was nothing which occurred at Calvary more strange and deeply mysterious, than the bitter exclamation which we have adopted as a text. Jesus had been so gloriously recognized and honored by His heavenly Father at His baptism, and on the mount of transfiguration, that we naturally feel astonished at His desertion in that most important and solemn of all moments, when He was yielding up the ghost, and sinking into the cold arms of mortality.

I. The Time and Circumstances of Messiah's Complaint.

A. *The time of Messiah's complaint.* It was afternoon. Jesus had now been suspended six hours upon the cross. He had been enduring an exceedingly painful, yet lingering death. Darkness had covered the whole land three hours. And it is supposed that during these three hours Jesus had not uttered a single sentence. At length the long silence is broken, and He exclaims, "My God," etc.

B. *The manner of His exclamation.* "He cried with a loud voice." Indicating that He was still possessed of full power; that nature was not, as in ordinary cases, exhausted. And that His life could not be forced from Him; but that He had power to lay it down, and also power to take it up again. As a sacrifice for sin, it was indispensably necessary that it should be His own free and voluntary act.

C. *His exclamation was that of Scripture prophecy.* Psalm 22. This was the case, also, when He commenced His ministry—when He was tempted—when reasoning with the Jews—when referring to His sufferings and death; Luke 24:46-48.

D. *It was language indicating His claim to the Messiahship.* He had ever professed to be the Son, the Savior of the world, been condemned for this and was now dying for this. And He still claims Jehovah as His God with His expiring breath, "My God, My God," etc.

E. *It was the only complaint He uttered upon the cross.* He did not complain of the apostasy of His friends—of the treachery of Judas—of Peter's denial—of Pilate's sentence—of the scourging. He did not complained when nailed to the wood: but when He felt the mental and spiritual darkness, He was overwhelmed, and and intense agony cried, "My God, My God," etc. Let us consider,

II. The Nature of His Complaint.

We are not to suppose that the divine was now separated from the human nature of Christ. Nor yet that God did not delight in Him and love Him as intensely as ever. Christ was never more dear and precious to the Father than at this time. But,

A. *He was now deprived of the joys of His Father's presence.* He was now offering up His soul as a sacrifice for sin. It, therefore, behooved Him to experience the dreadful penalty of sin. As man's Surety and Mediator, it was necessary that He should experience the judicial hidings of His Father's face.

B. *He had now completed all His engagements, and therefore claimed the approval of His Father.* It is generally thought that Christ's soul had been judicially forsaken for three hours. He now, therefore, appeals, as if He had said, O Father, the cup is now exhausted—the whole demand has been met: now let me have the token of your accepting love. "My God, My God," etc.

C. *After all, it was the cry of confidence.* He knew His unalienable interest in His Father's regard; and was satisfied that His Father always loved and therefore would always hear Him; He exclaimed, "My God, My God," etc. Let us consider,

III. **The Instruction Which We Derive from Christ's Complaint upon the Cross.**

A. *The ability and sufficiency of Christ as a Savior.* Jesus overcame singly all our and all His own adversaries. He proved Himself mighty to save.

B. *The qualification He possesses as our great High Priest.* He knows what poverty, temptation, calumny, persecution, death, and desertion mean.

C. *We learn the infinite evil of sin.* When Christ, as our substitute, had it pressing upon His holy soul, it caused Him to exclaim, "My God," etc.

D. *The essential value of God's reconciled countenance.* How necessary to us in life! but more so in adversity, in sickness, in death, and in eternity. Bless God! we may obtain it and enjoy it through faith in His Son. He is the way to the Father; and whosoever comes to God through Him, shall in no wise be cast out.

E. *The claims of Christ upon us.* What has He not a right to possess? He deserves our body, spirit, soul, our all, both in time and in eternity.

Let us then love, honor, and obey Him that at last we may join the heavenly hosts, and praise Him forever.

JABEZ BURNS

A VISIT TO THE TOMB OF CHRIST

"Come, see the place where the Lord lay" (Matt. 28:6).

Angels have often been employed to communicate important tidings to man. They often appeared to the patriarchs; conveyed intelligence to the prophets; announced the birth of the Savior; directed His escape into Egypt; ministered to Him in the desert; and doubtless watched with intense interest the events of the cross; and were the first to gladden the hearts of the devoted women, the friends of Jesus, by the cheering tidings of the text, "He is not here; for He is risen: come, see the place where the Lord lay."

I. The Person Referred to.
   "The Lord."
   While it is a most important blessed truth, that Christ really assumed our nature, and became our true kinsman; yet it is not less true or important, that He possessed a nature infinitely superior to ours; that He claimed equality with the Father; and that, as such, He bears the title of Lord, even "Lord of all."
   The propriety of this designation will appear from its application to Him,
   A. *By prophets.* There is a sublime representation of Him as such in Isaiah's vision (6:5-10); as quoted, also, John 12:41; see, also, Isaiah 40:3, and Jeremiah 23:6, and Psalm 68:16-18.
   B. *By the apostles and disciples.* Peter says, "He is Lord of all," (Acts 10:36). Paul describes Him as "Lord over all," (Rom. 10:12); "The Lord from heaven," (1 Cor. 15:47); "Lord of glory," (1 Cor. 2:8). John, in Revelation 17:14, "Lord of lords, and King of kings." The same title is given to Him,
   C. *By angels.* At His birth: "Unto you is born this day in the city of David, a Savior who is Christ the Lord." And also in the text: "Come, see the place where the Lord lay." It was received and assumed,
   D. *By Christ Himself.* The disciples invariably addressed Him by this title. He often spoke of Himself under the same. And He expressly says, "Ye call me Lord and Master, and say well" (John 13:13). The highest terms conceivable are addressed to Him,
   E. *By the Father.* "Thy throne, O God, is forever and ever," etc. And again: "And thou, Lord, in the beginning hast laid the foundation of the earth," etc. (Heb. 1:8-12).

II. The Place Where the Lord Lay.

It was the sepulcher. And there are many interesting circumstances connected with the place.

A. It was not His own; it belonged to another.

It is said, that the Jews were guilty of neglecting the interment of the poor; and, doubtless, the remains of criminals were often left to wither near the place of execution. This might have been their design in reference to Christ, had not Joseph of Arimathea begged for the body, and laid it in his own tomb; by which, also, an illustrious prophecy was fulfilled (Isa. 53:9).

B. *In this place He remained a certain predicted period.*

A period sufficient to prove His decease; and yet not sufficient to effect putrefaction. For, by the Psalmist, God had said, "He would not leave His soul in hell, nor suffer His Holy One to see corruption" (Ps. 16:10; Acts 2:31). Christ, also, had spoken to the same effect (Matt. 16:21; Luke 13:32).

C. *This place was carefully watched and powerfully guarded by His enemies.*

And by this the Christian has irrefragable evidence that Christ did rise from the dead, and never could have been secretly removed by His disciples. Never did the enemies of Jesus do Him better service, than when they rolled the mighty stone to the mouth of the tomb, sealed it with the imperial signet, and caused the spot to be watched by the Roman guard. The excuse made to the people, when Christ was not to be found, carries its own refutation (Matt. 28:65; 28:11, etc.).

D. *From this place Christ arose with power and glory.*

An angel descends from heaven; the stone is rolled away; an earthquake shakes the ground; the keepers tremble and become as dead men; the glory of the Lord surrounds the spot; death is overcome; and Christ arises, saying, "I am He that liveth, and was dead; and behold, I am alive forevermore" (Rev. 1:18).

III. The Lessons to Be Derived.

"Come, *see* the place where the Lord lay."

By a visit to the empty sepulcher we learn,

A. *That the mission of Jesus had been completed.*

He became the voluntary surety for the sinner. As such He endured the pain, bore the cure, becoming a curse for us. He gave His life as a ransom; the price was accepted, demanded, paid. He yields up His spirit and enters the region of the dead.

Prophecy is now fulfilled; justice has no further claim; the angel is sent to open the door of the prison, and the surety is liberated. By this, Christ's claim to the Messiahship is irrevocably established, and a firm foundation laid for the hope of the sinner.

B. *We learn that the enemies of Christ and of man are completely vanquished.*

Yes, death has been overcome in our nature, and in his own domains. The Conqueror has trampled upon all the powers of darkness. We learn,

C. *That the grave is a hallowed, sanctified place.*

Jesus has perfumed it with the fragrance of His own person. He has divested it of its natural gloom, and it now becomes the happy retreat of the worn-out pilgrim, where he can rest in happy quiet until the day of his full redemption. We learn,

D. *That the grave is only the temporary abode of the bodies of mankind.*

Its bars are now dislodged, and its chains broken. Adam forced an entrance into it; and the second Adam, the Lord from heaven, has made a passage through it. And through all its once dark and dreary extent there is now inscribed in glorious characters, "Christ has abolished death; and life and immortality are brought to light by the gospel." "Now is Christ risen from the dead, and become the first-fruits of them that slept." "Because I live, ye shall live also." We learn,

E. *Where we are to find Jesus.*

Not in Bethlehem, at Jordan, in the temple, or in the garden, on the cross, or in the sepulcher; no; He is now exalted at God's right hand, where He waits to dispense the blessings of His grace, to all who believe and call upon His name. "Let us, then, draw near with a true heart," etc. (Heb. 4:16 and 10:22).

Application
1. Come, skeptical sinner, and see the place where Christ lay; and admit His claims, and receive Him as the Son of God.

2. Come, mourning sinner, and see the place where Christ lay; and believe His ability to save you to the uttermost, seeing He ever lives to make intercession for you.

3. Come, timid believer, and see the place where Christ lay; and be not kept in bondage, through the fear of death. It is your privilege to exclaim, "O death, where is thy sting? O grave, where is thy victory?"   JABEZ BURNS

THE PHARISEES' TAUNT

"This man receiveth sinners" (Luke 15:2).

It was Christ's lot to be misunderstood and ridiculed. The purity and nobility of His life counted as nothing, because He did not conform to the habits and practices of those around Him.

I. **The Conduct Complained of.**
"This man receiveth *sinners*"; i.e., outcasts.

A. But why were they outcasts? Were those who despised and spurned them better than they? "The publicans and the harlots enter heaven before you."

During the reign of law, the doctrine was: "once lost, lost forever." Christ instituted the reign of mercy.

B. But had not the Pharisees reason to complain? Might it not have been expected that Christ would choose different associates from these? Might it not be said that "Like draws like"?

Their prejudices were awakened.
Their pride was wounded.
Their belief in His Messiahship was shaken.

II. **The Explanation of Christ's Conduct.**
"They that are whole need not a physician, but they that are sick. I came not to call the righteous," etc.

He was in His right place.

The physician is expected to be among the sick and the dying; the teacher, among the ignorant; the philanthropist, among the wretched; the missionary, among the darkened and depraved.

He received sinners, but,
Not as equals.
Not with approbation.
Only to do them good.
Observe:
A. The intensity of His compassion.
B. The purity of His motives.
C. The greatness of His self-sacrificing love.

SELECTED

HEROD AND CHRIST

"He sent Him to Herod" (Luke 23:7).

Why? It may have been a simple act of courtesy. This is the reason assigned: "As soon as He knew that He belonged to Herod's jurisdiction." But it is probable, also, that He wished to rid Himself of the responsibility of condemning an innocent man.

I. Herod's Gladness at the Sight of Christ.
   Why was He glad?
   Not because he wanted to reform his character.
   Not because he wanted stronger evidence of Christ's Messiahship.
   Not because he wanted spiritual instruction.
   Not because he wanted to do Him justice.
   But because he wanted his curiosity gratified and his intolerable boredom relieved.

II. Herod's Treatment of Christ.
   "He questioned Him with many words." Flippant, unprofitable questions, to which no answer would be given.
   "Herod and his men of war set Him at naught," etc., irritated, no doubt, by His determined silence. But the intended insult was a real honor: unwittingly he arrayed Christ in the garb worn by the high priest on the day of atonement.

III. Herod's Reconciliation with Pilate Through the Trial of Christ.
   "The same day Pilate and Herod were made friends together," etc.
   The cause of the quarrel may have been Pilate's massacre of the Galileans (Luke 13:1). Their common hostility to Christ was the ground of their renewed friendship.
   Sin is often a bond of union among men.
   The most opposite characters are united in opposing Christ.
   Such friendship is not lasting.
   Christ stood at Herod's tribunal; now Herod must be judged by Christ.

SELECTED

THE CRUCIFIXION

"And when they were come to the place called Calvary, there they crucified Him, and the malefactors; one on the right hand, and the other on the left" (Luke 23:33).

How striking is the contrast between the conduct of Jesus, and that of His enemies. When they were come to Calvary, there they crucified Him; and while they crucified Him, He prayed for His murderers, saying, "Father, forgive them; for they know not what they do" (v. 34).

In offering a few remarks upon the text, there are three things particularly worthy of notice—the place where our Lord suffered—the nature of His sufferings—and the company in which He suffered.

I. Observe the Place Where He Suffered.

This is called Calvary, or Golgotha, a small eminence, about half a mile distant from Jerusalem. This was the common place of execution, where the worst offenders were put to death.

Two things may be observed concerning this, one relating to the intention of the murderers, and the other showing the intention of the writer:

A. The place where Jesus suffered, marks *the malignant design of His enemies.* It was not without some reason on their part that they fixed on Calvary; it was to render His name and character infamous, to express the greatest abhorrence of both, to sink and ruin His cause by affixing an indelible disgrace. Hence it was that the cross of Christ became a stumbling block to the Jews, and to the Greeks, foolishness. But in this they were ultimately disappointed.

B. The place as mentioned by the evangelist *marks his strong affection.* The sacred writer employs but few words, his narration is slow and solemn, and expressive of the deepest feelings of the heart. He points to the spot with peculiar emphasis, as Jacob did to the field of Machpelah, saying, *"There* they buried Abraham and Sarah his wife; there they buried Isaac and Rebekah his wife; and there I buried Leah" (Gen. 49:31). Another instance of this form of speech occurs in the address of Ruth to Naomi: "Where thou diest, will I die, and *there* will I be buried" (Ruth 1:17). Thus the evangelist points to Calvary, and with deep emotion says, *"There* they crucified Him."

C. We may also add that this directs us to *the place where we must look for mercy*. There they crucified Him, and thence our salvation comes. There the great sacrifice was offered up, the ransom price paid, and the great atonement made.

II. The Nature of His Sufferings: "They crucified Him."

The sin of which the Jews pretended to accuse our Lord, was that of blasphemy, because that "He being a man, made Himself God; and calling God His Father, He made Himself equal with God." By the Jewish law a blasphemer was to be stoned to death, and therefore they took up stones to cast at Him; but being at that time under the Roman government, they had no power to put anyone to death. They therefore brought Him before Pilate, demanding that He should be crucified. The Roman law inflicted capital punishment by various other means, chiefly by decapitation; but crucifixion was fixed upon to gratify the wrath of the Jews, and the unrighteous judge yielded to their wishes. In all this the hand of God may be traced, and His wisdom seen in overruling these events for the accomplishment of His own purposes.

A. The death of the cross, though selected by Jewish anger, would be *the fulfillment of prophecy*. The disciples were blind to these things when they happened, but afterward they saw plainly that thus it was written, and that thus it behooved Christ to suffer. Prophecy had foretold that they should pierce His hands and His feet (Ps. 22:16); and also His side (Zech. 12:10; John 19:34, 37). Our Lord also had Himself foretold, in numerous instances, that He should be betrayed into the hands of sinners, and be crucified (John 3:14; 8:28; 12:32,33). He had also rendered the idea familiar by calling a profession of His name, with all the difficulties attending it, a bearing of the cross, in allusion to His carrying the cross of Calvary (Matt. 16:24; Mark 10:21; Luke 19:23). Hence also the doctrine of Christ crucified, as the only medium of our salvation, formed the very essence of the gospel itself (1 Cor. 2:2; Gal. 3:1; 6:14).

B. In our Lord's suffering the death of the cross, there was something *analogous to what we as sinners had deserved*; and probably it was with a view to represent this, that the Jews were allowed to crucify Him.

1. It was a *lingering death*, and the Romans appear to have invented this mode of punishment on purpose to render death as dreadful as possible. In the case of our blessed Lord it was six hours, from the commencement to the end of the crucifixion, when,

having power to lay down His life, He voluntarily gave up the ghost; but the thieves had not then expired, and would probably have survived many hours longer (Mark 15:44; John 19:33). All this time the sufferer would experience the most horrible thirst, from all the extreme anguish so long endured (Pss. 22:15; 69:21; John 19:28). And in this lengthened pain and anguish there was something that represented the endless punishment of the wicked.

2. It was a most *painful death*, more so perhaps than any other that human malignity could devise. The wounds were all inflicted on the tenderest parts of the human body, but not so as to effect the seat of life. In the act of fixing the cross in the ground, with the sufferer suspended on it, His joints would be dislocated by the shock; and thus another prophecy would be fulfilled (Ps. 22:14). These exquisite sufferings would shadow forth those torments of hell, in which the sinner shall thirst in vain for water to cool his tongue, and where the ever burning sulfur is unconsumed.

3. The death of the cross was attended with *reproach and infamy*; none so painful, so ignominious as this. He was made a spectacle to angels and to men, and they that passed by wagged the head in derision and contempt. Yet He endured the cross, and despised the shame. In this also there was a prefiguration of that public disgrace and overwhelming shame, which the righteous judge has awarded as the punishment of sin (Dan. 12:2, Isa. 66:24).

4. The death of the cross was an *accursed death*, both in the esteem of God and man (Gal. 3:13). And the sentence to which sinners are doomed is, that they are to die the death, to die under the curse. Hence Jesus would come under the law, and into our place and stead, and so was made a curse for us.

III. The Company in Which He Suffered: "Two Malefactors, One on the Right Hand, and the Other on the Left."

A. On the part of His enemies this was designed to render His death still *more ignominious and shameful*, and was no doubt contrived between Pilate and the chief priests. Our blessed Lord was holy, harmless and undefiled, and separate from sinners; but now to overwhelm Him with shame and public disgrace, they associate Him with "malefactors." Not content with this, they place Him in the midst, to insinuate that He was the worst of the three. This arrangement might also be contrived for the purpose of, during His last moments, by filling His ear with the blasphemies and reproaches of His dying companions. When we come to die, the least comfort we hope for is a peaceful pillow, and the presence of a sympathizing friend. But here is the blessed Savior, surrounded by an enraged populace, and expiring on the cross, amidst the execrations of His enemies, and the groans of dying criminals.

B. But on the part of God we may see something of *the wisdom of this appointment*. Prophecy was hereby fulfilled, which said that He should be numbered with transgressors (Isa. 53:11; Mark 15:27,28). By this means also the virtue of His sacrifice was made more fully apparent. Had two of His disciples been crucified with Him, instead of two thieves, it might have been imagined that they had contributed something to the efficacy of His sufferings: but as it is, it would appear that His own arm brought salvation, and His righteousness sustained Him. He trod the winepress alone, and of the people there was none with Him (Isa. 63).

C. Also by suffering in such society, an opportunity was given for the fuller display of His power and grace, in saving one of the malefactors in His last moments, and taking Him from the cross to the paradise of God. Moreover, the publicity of His crucifixion rendered the evidence of His death more certain and indisputable, so that His enemies could not pretend that there was any collusion and it established the reality of His death, established also the reality of His subsequent resurrection, on which all the hopes of His followers depend.

CONDENSED FROM CHARLES SIMEON

CHRIST'S INTERCESSION ON THE CROSS

"Then said Jesus, Father, forgive them; for they know not what they do" (Luke 23:34).

What a surprising contrast, between the treatment which the blessed Savior received from His enemies, and that which they received from Him in return (v. 33).

We see here the wisdom of God overruling the enmity of wicked men. They crucify Jesus, to render His name infamous; and place Him between two thieves to cover Him with reproach. But by this lingering, painful, and shameful death, an opportunity was given for the Savior more fully to express His love. While suspended on the cross He uttered many things and all of them highly interesting and important. Here also He made intercession for the transgressors.

I. Observe the Petition Itself: "Father, Forgive Them."
    How well this agrees with prophecy (Isa. 53:12).
    A. Notice *the magnitude of the blessing* prayed for, even "forgiveness." This includes all other blessings, and an interest in eternal life. Sin is the great mountain that stands between God and us, and prevents the manifestation of His favor; if that be removed, all is removed. It is forgiveness that extracts the sting of death, and calms the terrors of a future judgment; for if God forgives, who is He that shall condemn? Forgiveness takes away the curse of the law, and the bitterness of all affliction in this life. In the present instance especially, it is a blessing greater than could be asked or thought by any other than the blessed Redeemer Himself.
    B. Consider *the extreme unworthiness of the objects*. Surely, if such be pardoned, it must indeed be according to the riches of His grace. They were not common sinners, nor had they committed any common offense: they had killed the Prince of life, and crucified the Lord of glory. They had put Him to open shame whom God had made heir of all things, and by whom also He made the worlds. To pray for such sinners was love operating against hatred, and doing good against evil in the highest sense possible. He had met with enough from their hands to turn His heart against them; but His was love that many waters could not quench, neither could the floods drown it. Such is His love to us also; for when we were enemies He died for us, and it is wholly owing to His intercession that we are spared and pardoned (Rom. 5:10).

C. The *heinous nature of their offense*: "they know not what they do." This very plea implies that it was an awful sin they were committing, though they were blinded to it; it was one on which the heavens frowned with preternatural darkness, and the earth trembled while they perpetrated the dreadful deed. It was such as might have awakened the vengeance of God, to send out evil spirits and destroy them. For offering insult to an angel in human form, the inhabitants of Sodom were smitten with blindness; but the guilt of the inhabitants of Jerusalem is not to be described.

D. The *efficacy of the petition*, in securing the blessing prayed for. A good man might say of his murderers as Stephen did, "Lord, lay not this sin to their charge"; but it would not follow that they would certainly be forgiven. But the intercession of Christ is forever prevalent, for Him the Father hears always. The blood which then flowed from the cross gave efficacy to His prayer; the plea itself was the cry of blood, even of that which speaks better things than the blood of Abel. The plea of the suffering Savior had an immediate reference to His death, the very design of which was to procure the forgiveness of sin. In this instance therefore He showed what was the object of His sacrifice, and how it would be carried into effect by His intercession (Luke 24:46,47).

II. The Plea by Which the Petition Is Enforced: "They Know Not What They Do."

A. It is such as would *have not been found by any other advocate*. Who indeed could have devised any plea whatever for such an offense, and for such sinners; or who dared so much as to think of a plea in such a case! Yet the blessed Savior finds one, and the only one that could avail (1 Tim. 1:13).

B. It is a plea which shows *that sin has different degrees of guilt*, according to the circumstances under which it is committed. Sins committed through ignorance and unbelief, though great, are not so aggravated as those committed against light and knowledge: hence it was that Paul obtained mercy, while apostates find none (1 Tim. 1:13; Heb. 10:26-29). Heathens, though guilty, are not so fearfully involved as those who have the gospel and reject it (Heb. 2:3, 12:25).

C. It is a plea which teaches us that *for some there was no mercy*, though there might be for those on whose behalf it was offered. There is a sin unto death, which has no forgiveness in this world, nor in that which is to come (Matt. 12:32). And there were some among the Jews for whom there was no mercy for what they had done, though the populace in general, and many of the rulers, knew not what they did; and hence it was that Peter afterward exhorted them to repentance, in the hope of their being forgiven (Acts 3:17-19).

D. Though their ignorance afforded a plea for mercy, *they were not to be pardoned without repentance*. Christ never prayed that sinners should be forgiven only in this way, nor that they should be pardoned before they repent, for this would be incompatible with the whole design of His mediation. His intercession for their pardon therefore includes repentance, and hence it was that such multitudes of the Jews were afterwards pricked to the heart under Peter's sermon (Acts 2:37). Sinners must know what they have done, before they can expect mercy (Jer. 2:19).

Summary

1. We see there is that in the nature of sin which surpasses all our conceptions. When sinners offend against God, oppose the gospel, and reject the Savior, "they know not what they do." Would anyone, if he knew it, offend his best friend, serve his worst enemy, and plunge himself into endless ruin? Or having brought himself into danger, would he reject the way of escape! Yet such is the case with every unbeliever.

2. Still we learn that notwithstanding the evil nature of sin, there is no reason for despair, not even for the chief of sinners. If Jerusalem sinners can be pardoned, there is hope for all: and it was amongst these unparalleled offenders that the mercy was to begin, as an example to all nations (Luke 24:47).

3. The conduct of our blessed Lord is set before us in this instance as an example, teaching us what must be our spirit toward our enemies and persecutors. Stephen followed this example, and we must learn to do the same (Acts 7:60, Matt. 5:44,45).

CONDENSED FROM CHARLES SIMEON

"Thus it is written, and thus it behooved Christ to suffer, and to rise from the dead the third day: and that repentance, and remission of sins should be preached in His name, among all nations, beginning at Jerusalem" (Luke 24:46,47).

It is remarkable how discouraged the disciples were before the resurrection of Christ. That event was like a resurrection to them, and by it they were begotten again to a lively hope (1 Peter 1:3).

1. Observe, the words of our Lord, addressed to His disciples, were intended to set their hearts at rest; by showing them that nothing had taken place but what was foretold in the Scriptures, and predetermined of God. His plan was going on, whatever were the designs of men. This was like setting their feet on a rock when they were sinking: this truth they also remembered, and afterwards employed to an important purpose (Acts 2:23; 4:28).

2. The words were also designed to explain to them so much as they immediately needed, and no more. There were other things that it behooved Christ to do, as well as to suffer: it behooved Him to ascend to heaven, to reign, to intercede, to come again. But this was not their present concern, and there-fore His death and resurrection only are mentioned.

I. Notice the Great and Interesting Facts which had lately transpired, and had filled the minds of the disciples with so much distress.

It was a fact then, that Christ had suffered—had risen again—and furnished them with a message of salvation.

A. *Christ had suffered,* had expired on the cross. This was an event on which all our salvation depended.

How did He suffer, and in what capacity? As a *martyr*? This is true, though not the whole truth. He did suffer indeed that He might bear witness to the truth, and for this cause came He into the world (John 18:37).

But this was not the principal cause of His sufferings and death: He suffered and died as a *substitute* in our stead. He was made sin for us, who Himself knew no sin: He died for us, and bore our sins in His own body on the tree (1 Cor. 15:3; 2 Cor. 5:21; 1 Peter 2:24).

As a *martyr* only, He suffered from the hands of wicked men; but as a *substitute*, He suffered from the hands of God. "It pleased the Lord to bruise Him, and put His soul to grief." He bore the divine displeasure due to us. He complained not of the former, but "endured the cross, despising the shame." But in the latter case He felt and expressed Himself in the strongest language (Matt. 2:38,39). Job complained that his grief was heavier than the sand; and the church in captivity exclaimed, What meaneth the heat of this great anger. But all this was as nothing compared with what Christ suffered, for He was made a curse for us (Deut. 29:23,24; Lam. 3:1; Gal. 3:13).

B. *He had risen again*. This was another fact which had taken place; He had obtained a victory over the grave, and was loosed from the bands of death. God had raised Him up, according to the working of His mighty power, and this in token of His approval and acceptance of His sacrifice. Yes, He is risen indeed, and has appeared unto Simon. This was the source of a lively hope, and an example of our own resurrection.

C. He had furnished His apostles with a *message of salvation*. This is called "preaching repentance, and remission of sins, among all nations." This was another important fact, which should soon be realized.

1. Observe, *repentance* was not itself followed by *remission*, as a necessary consequence: sin was too heinous to be thus atoned for. Repentance is the duty of all mankind. But through the mediation of Christ, repentance and remission are now joined together. Now, if we confess our sins, He is faithful and just to forgive us our sins: but this connection is all of grace.

2. The remission of sins is joined with repentance, but through the name of Jesus, that remission of sins is granted, and there is none in any other way (1 John 1:7, 9).

3. This message of mercy is sent to *all nations*, "beginning at Jerusalem." This was now the worst city in all the world, for there they had crucified the Lord of life and glory. Yet there the mercy was to begin, though it was not to end there. Such was the fullness of Christ's sacrifice, that its blessings should be extended to all nations.

II. Consider the Necessity There Was for These Things Taking Place.

It was necessary, in particular, that Christ should suffer, and rise again from the dead, and that on two accounts:

A. It was necessary *from the Scriptures of truth*: "thus it is written." Moses and the prophets had all foretold that He should suffer and rise again (v. 44). The seed of the woman (Gen. 3:16); Abraham's lamb for sacrifice, the prophecies of David in Psalms 22 and 59, and those of Isaiah 53 all predicted this event. So also His resurrection had been foretold (Ps. 16). He should see His seed, prolong His days, and the pleasure of the Lord should prosper in His hands.

B. It was also necessary *from the nature of things*. "It behooved Him to suffer"; it was not possible that the cup should pass from Him (Matt. 24:39; Luke 24:26; Heb. 2:17; 10:4). Yet it may be asked, in what sense did it behoove Him to suffer? Certainly He was not originally obliged to it: no, it behooved us as sinners to suffer, and not Him. We should have suffered justly, had we been consigned to punishment: but this cannot be said of our Surety. It is only in consideration of two things that it behooved Him to suffer:

1. His own voluntary *engagements*. There was a necessity for His going through with the work which He had begun: He had sworn as it were to His own hurt, but repentance must be hid from His eyes.

2. Our *salvation* made it necessary. If we be saved, the cup must not pass from Him; otherwise God would have spared His own Son. He must bear the curse, or it must fall upon us: He must drink the cup, or we cannot be exempt.

It was also fit that He should *rise again*: for if not risen, we are yet in our sins. His sacrifice would not have availed, had He not risen to carry it into effect: hence it is said that He died for our sins, and was raised again for our justification: and hence it is that He is able also to save to the uttermost (Rom. 4:25; 5:10; Heb. 7:25).

There was likewise a propriety in *repentance being preached in His name*. It was fit that pardon should then be proclaimed: the jubilee followed on the great day of atonement (Lev. 25:9). It was not for the sake of repentance, but for His name's sake: yet without repentance there is no remission.

Application

1. We learn from this the way of salvation: "repent and believe the gospel." This is the way for all men and for all nations to the end of time, and no other way will do.

2. We see the all-sufficiency of salvation for the chief of sin-

ners. The gospel might first have been sent to other nations, and last of all to the Jews: but to display its fullness it was to "begin" at Jerusalem.

3. The deplorable condition of those who perish in unbelief, and from under the sound of mercy (Matt. 23:37).

CHARLES SIMEON

THREE CROSSES OF CALVARY

The men who were associated with Christ are an object lesson for us as to the difference there is between the believer and the unbeliever in relation to the question of sin. Let us look at the three men.

Upon the center cross is Christ. Is there sin *in* Him? No. He did no sin (1 Peter 2:22); He knew no sin (2 Cor. 5:21); and in Him was no sin (1 John 3:5).

Was there sin *on* Him? Yes. For God made to meet upon Him the iniquity of us all (Isa. 53:6, M.).

Was there sin *in* the thieves? Yes. For they were, like all, conceived in sin (Ps. 51:5).

Was there sin *on* the thieves? Yes, and no.

Upon the believing thief there was no sin, for Christ was his Sin-Bearer.

Upon the unbelieving thief there was sin, for he did not look to Christ for salvation from it.

Believing thief	Christ	Unbelieving thief
Sin in him.	Sin not in Him.	Sin in him.
No sin on him.	Sin on Him.	Sin on him.

The relation to Christ of the thieves made all the difference as to their state before God. So is it now. They who believe in Christ have their sins borne away by Christ (1 Peter 2:24), and those who do not are rewarded according to their works (Rev. 20:12).

F. E. MARSH

"Behold the Lamb of God, who takes away the sin of the world" *(John 1:29).*

The death of our Lord Jesus Christ, considered as the only saving remedy for a perishing world, demands our serious attention every day in the year; but on that particular day which is set apart by the Christian church for the commemoration of His last sufferings, we should examine the subject with deep reverence. The results of our examinations will amply repay our careful and diligent inquiries; for thereby we shall gain clear views of a subject, which of all others, is the most important to man; we shall feel ourselves deeply humbled before God, under a sense of those sins which nailed our Savior to the tree, and our drooping spirits will be revived and cheered with a hope of salvation, by Him who suffered on the cross. Our text points out Christ as the Lamb of God; affirms that He takes away the sin of the world; and exhorts sinful men to behold Him.

I. Jesus Christ Is the Lamb of God.

A. *The paschal Lamb was a type of Christ.* A parallel might be drawn in many important particulars; but we shall only mention one: by the death of that lamb, and the sprinkling of its blood upon the door posts, all the firstborn of Israel were saved from death (Ex. 12:6,7); and we are assured that "even Christ our passover is sacrificed for us" (1 Cor. 5:7); and by His death, and the sprinkling of His blood, we are saved from wrath (Rom. 5:9).

B. *But Jesus is called the Lamb of God, especially in reference to the daily sacrifice,* which was offered up every morning and evening continually, and was a standing type of Him (Ex. 29:38,39). The lambs which were offered in the daily sacrifice were to be without blemish, and our Savior was without sin (1 Peter 1:19); they made a *typical* atonement, but He made a *real* atonement (1 John 2:2); they were *imperfect*; but our Lord was but once offered, being an *all-perfect* offering and sacrifice (Heb. 9:25,26).

C. *The prophet Isaiah foretold the Jewish nation that the Messiah would be brought as a lamb to the slaughter,* and that "as a sheep before her shearers is dumb, so He would not open His mouth" (53:7). In this prediction, two things are clearly stated, first, the death of Jesus as a slaughtered lamb; and, secondly, His patience in that awful scene. He was manifested in the flesh to destroy the works of the devil (1 John 3:8); and to accomplish that, "it behooved Him to suffer, and to rise from the dead" (Luke 24:46).

D. *Jesus now appears, as a lamb slain, in the heavenly world* (Rev. 5:6). That appearance, in all probability, is intended to remind glorified human spirits of their salvation by His atonement; and hence, while this great truth is denied by some on earth, it is celebrated with songs of praise, by the redeemed of the Lord (v. 8); and they ascribe to the Lamb who redeemed them, power and riches, strength and honor, and glory and blessing (v. 12).

E. *Other things are affirmed of Jesus, as an atoning Lamb, which prove the propriety of this name.* The sanctification of the saints in heaven is ascribed to His blood, where it is said, they "have washed their robes and made them white in the blood of the Lamb"; they overcame the accuser by the blood of the Lamb; and they are made kings and priests unto God, by His blood (Rev. 7:14; 12:11; 1:5, 6).

II. He Takes Away the Sin of the World.

A. *The sin of Adam in the garden of Eden affected the whole world of mankind* (Rom. 5:17-21; 1 Cor. 15:21); but it is so far taken away by the Lamb of God, that all will rise from death, and none will suffer in the eternal world for what He did (1 Cor. 15:22; Ezek. 18:20).

B. *But by the sin of the world is meant all the sins of men, whether Jews or Gentiles;* including every kind of sin, unless we may except that against the Holy Spirit (Matt. 12:32); and every degree of sin; a remedy is provided for all who go astray (Isa. 53:6).

C. *Jesus takes away sin, by the sacrifice of Himself once offered* (Heb. 10:12; 1 Peter 3:18); and all the sin which is taken away is through His precious blood (Heb. 9:32); for no man can remove His own sin from His conscience, nor can any man take away the sin of His brother, or give a ransom for Him (Ps. 45:7); neither is there salvation in any other name than that of Jesus (Acts 4:12).

D. *When men repent and believe the gospel, the guilt of their sin is taken away by the Lamb of God;* and they are justified, accepted, and adopted into the family of God (Mark 1:15; Rom. 5:1; Eph. 1:6; Rom. 8:16).

E. *By faith the pollution of sin is taken away.* It is expressly affirmed that we are sanctified by faith in Christ Jesus (Acts 25:18); that our hearts are purified by faith (Acts 15:9); and that "the blood of Jesus Christ cleanseth us from all sin" (1 John 1:7).

F. *Through Jesus the Lamb of God, the practice of sin is taken away:* hence His followers excel in all holy conversation and godliness (2 Peter 3:11); for He saves them from their sins (Matt. 1:21). Being saved by grace, they deny "ungodliness and worldly lusts," and "live . . . godly in this present world" (Titus 2:12).

G. *The tormenting fears which accompany sin are taken away by the Lamb of God, from all who are perfected in love* (1 John 4:18); so that they are no longer tormented, like other men, with frightful fears of death and hell, but rejoice in hope of the glory of God (Rom. 5:2).

H. *The sad effects of sin in a future state will be taken away by the Lamb of God from all who die in the Lord* (Rev. 14:13). They will have a blessed and glorious resurrection (1 Cor. 15:51,52); they will appear with boldness in the day of judgment (1 John 4:17); and they will "be forever with the Lord" (1 Thess. 4:18).

I. *All the sin which was taken away before Christ suffered for men was taken away by Him.* He was to be the Savior, and when the first promise was made, the gospel day began to dawn (Gen. 3:15). From that day to this, men have been placed in His hands, as the only Mediator; and through His grace, the channels of mercy were opened immediately after the fall of our first parents.

J. *And if sin be taken away in the heathen world, it is by the Lamb of God*; for, through His blood, they may come "from the east and from the west, and from the north and from the south, and sit down in the kingdom of God" (Luke 6:29). Thus "in every nation, he that feareth God and worketh righteousness, is accepted," through Him who died for all (Acts 10:35).

III. Sinful Men Are Exhorted to Behold Him.

A. *The person to whom these words were addressed by John the Baptist, beheld the Savior with eyes of flesh*; for He was present among them, in His human body. In this sense we cannot see Him, because He has gone to the Father (John 16:28).

B. *But we behold Him by the eye of faith*, which enables us to look at things which are not seen by the natural eye (2 Cor. 4:18); but all the internal views of the mind must be directed by that which is revealed in the written Word, or we shall fall into foolish imaginations (2 Cor. 10:5).

C. *To behold Him as a religious duty is to believe in Him and to trust in Him for salvation* (Isa. 45:22); and this is not merely one act of the mind, at some certain period of our lives, but a continued act, expressed by *looking* to Jesus (Heb. 12:2).

D. Behold Him in His *birth* at Bethlehem, in His *holy life* among the wicked Jews, in His *death* on Mount Calvary, in His *resurrection* from the dead, and in His *ascension* to heaven, where "He ever liveth to make intercession" (Heb. 7:25). Contemplate these wonderful events, as they are recorded in the *Book*.

E. *Carefully behold Him in His sacred offices.* He was a prophet to guide us into all truth (Acts 3:22,23); a Priest to atone and intercede (Heb. 4:14); and a King to govern and protect us (Rev. 17:14; 19:16). Proper views of these offices will cheer your hearts, strengthen your hands, and inspire you with a blessed hope.

F. *As Christian believers, behold Him in His person.* He "is over all, God blessed forever" (Rom. 9:5); He is man, in the proper sense of the word, having a reasonable soul, and a body which died and rose again (Luke 2:52); and He is God-man, and Mediator between God and men (1 Tim. 2:5).

G. *It becomes us to behold Him with profound humility.* He had no sin of His own, either original or actual (Heb. 7:26); but He suffered for our sins, and was "wounded for our transgressions" (Isa. 53:5); this thought should lay us in the dust.

H. *But behold Him with grateful feelings.* We love Him because He is lovely; but, especially, because He first loved us (1 John 4:19). We should have been lost, and what but love could have moved Him to die for us? (Rom. 5:8).

I. *Hence we may behold Him with entire confidence.* His love is a proof that He is willing to save us; and we know "He is able to save to the uttermost" (Heb. 7:25). He offers salvation (Acts 13:26); He invites us to go to Him (Matt. 11:28); and He knocks at the door of our hearts (Rev. 3:20).

J. *While we view Him as our Savior, let us also behold Him as our exemplar.* There are good examples among men, but they are all imperfect; the example of Jesus should be placed before our eyes in all states and circumstances of life; and we should endeavor to imitate Him, as far as may be proper, in all our works, and in all our ways. To try to imitate Him in all things would be rash presumption; but while we follow His hospitality, meekness, patience, zeal, love and obedience, we shall be both safe and happy (1 Peter 2:21).

We conclude by observing, that all who thus behold the Lamb of God, shall see Him at the end of the world with great joy; that they shall meet Him in the air, and that they shall remain with Him as their bridegroom, in a blessed and glorious state of immortality (Rev. 21:2-9).

CONDENSED FROM CHARLES SIMEON

CHRIST THE RESURRECTION AND THE LIFE

"Jesus said unto her, I am the resurrection and the life: he that believeth in Me, though he were dead, yet shall he live: and whosoever liveth and believeth in Me, shall never die" (John 11:25,26).

In our text we have an account of a heavy affliction that had befallen a family, through the death of one, to whom Jesus had shown a very peculiar attachment. He had been asked to come and help them; but He had delayed His visit till Lazarus had been dead four days. This however, though liable to misconstruction, He had done intentionally, that He might manifest more fully to the disconsolate sisters His own power and glory. Accordingly, when they intimated their persuasion, that, if He would pray to God for the restoration of their brother to life, God would grant His request, He told them that He needed not beseech God to effect it; for that He Himself was the resurrection and the life: and was able to impart either bodily or spiritual life to whomsoever He would.

In considering this most remarkable declaration, we shall notice:

I. That Which Relates to Himself.

Martha having, in conformity with the prevailing opinion of the Jews, expressed her expectation of a general resurrection at the last day, Jesus says to her, "I am the resurrection."

Our Lord, in His divine nature, possessed omnipotence necessarily, and of Himself. In His mediatorial capacity He was invested with it by His Father, agreeably to the plan concerted in the divine counsels. To Him who had undertaken to procure salvation for a fallen world, was delegated all power requisite for the full discharge of that office. The restoring of His people to a new and heavenly life after death, was essential to their complete salvation: this therefore was committed to Him (John 5:21, 25-29); and He both declared He would execute this great work (John 6:39,40), and gave an earnest of its accomplishments in raising Himself from the dead (John 10:18; 1 Cor. 15:20).

"I am the life." In this term our Lord proceeds further than in the former, and asserts that as He is the author and first-fruits of the resurrection, so is He the very principle of life whereby His people live. Many figurative expressions of Scripture represent Him as the fountain of life to all His people (John 15:1; Eph. 4:15,16); but we are not left to gather such an important truth from mere parables; it is asserted frequently in the plainest terms: He is a quickening spirit (1 Cor. 15:45), that liveth in us (John 14:6; 6:57; Gal. 2:20), and is our very life (Col. 3:4). He is to the soul what the soul is to the body; He pervade, animates, and invigorates all our spiritual faculties: by His secret energy our understanding is enabled to apprehend divine truth, our will inclined to obey it: and, without Him, the soul would be as dead as the body without the soul.

II. That Which Respects His People.

There is a remarkable correspondence between the two latter, and the two former clauses of the text; the latter declaring the operation of the powers expressed in the former.

A. As being "the resurrection," He will raise the bodies of His people. Using our weak reason, we are ready to think that the restoration of bodies, which may have undergone so many changes, is impossible. But cannot He who formed the universe out of nothing, collect the atoms that constitute our identity, and reunite them to their kindred souls? He can, and will; yea, that very Jesus, who died upon the cross, has the keys of death and hell (Rev. 1:18), and will effect this by His own almighty power (Phil. 3:21).

This clause might further declare, that by the first act of faith in Him our souls should be made partakers of spiritual life. And this would accord with other passages of Scripture (John 6:33, 35; 7:38; 11:10), and prepare us for the next clause, which declares the benefits that shall result from a continued life of faith upon Him.

B. As being "the life," He will preserve the souls of His people unto everlasting life.

The bodies of the saints must undergo the sentence denounced against sin (Rom. 8:10); [though death to *them* is scarcely worthy the name of death: it is rather a sleep, from which they shall be awakened at the morning of the resurrection (v. 11; Acts 7:60; 1 Thess. 4:14)], but their souls shall never die: none shall prevail against them (Isa. 54:17); none shall pluck them out of Christ's hands (John 10:28); their life is hid in Him beyond the reach of men or devils (Col. 3:3); the vital principle within them is an ever-living seed (1 Peter 1:23), an over-flowing fountain (John 4:14); as long as Christ lives, they shall live also (John 14:19). The separation that will take place between their souls and bodies will only introduce them to a higher state of existence, which they shall enjoy until the day that their bodies shall be reunited.

We must not, however, fail to notice the description given of those to whom these promises are made.

Twice, in these few words, are these blessings limited to believers: not because our Lord disregards good works, or because they shall not be rewarded; but because we cannot do any good work unless we first receive strength from Christ by faith (John 15:5); and because, if we obtained life by working, we should be able to glory before God: and God has decreed that no flesh shall glory in His presence, and that we shall glory only in the Lord (Rom. 3:27; Eph. 2:8,9; 1 Cor. 1:29-31). It must never be forgotten that God has caused all fullness to dwell in His Son, Jesus Christ (Col. 1:19); and that we must, by a continued exercise of faith, receive out of that fullness grace for grace (John 1:16). It is by faith that we live (Gal. 3:11), we stand (2 Cor. 1:24), we walk (2 Cor. 5:7), we are saved (Gal. 2:16); in a word, "God has given us eternal life; but this life is *in His Son*; He therefore that hath the Son, hath life; and He that hath not the Son of God, hath not life" (1 John 5:11,12).

The pointed interrogation with which our Lord closed this address to Martha directs us how to *improve* this subject: it suggests:

1. That all persons, however eminent in their profession, or decided in their character, ought to "examine themselves whether they be in the faith."

2. That the believing of this record is the most effectual antidote against the troubles of life, or the fears of death. If Martha had felt the full influence of these truths, she would have moderated her sorrows, under the persuasion that her loss was her brother's gain; and that, if her brother were not restored to life, she should soon meet him in a better world. Thus in every state the consideration of these truths will afford to us also unspeakable consolation: for, if we believe in Christ, and have through Him the possession of spiritual, and the prospect of eternal life, what cause can we have to complain; what cause to fear? The world will be divested of its allurements, and death of its terrors. Satisfied that all events are under the control of our best friend, we shall commit them cheerfully to His wise disposal: and looking forward to the day in which He will call us from our graves, we shall expect His summons with composure at least, if not also with a holy impatience. Let us then live by faith on our divine Savior, assured that He will keep us unto eternal life, and exalt us, both in body and soul, unto the everlasting enjoyment of His presence and glory.

CONDENSED FROM CHARLES SIMEON

THE EFFECTS OF CHRIST'S DEATH

Now is the judgment of this world: now shall the prince of this world be cast out. And I, if [when-NIV] I be lifted up from the earth, will draw all men unto me (John 12:31,32).

Inconceivably arduous was the work that Christ had undertaken. Yet amidst His heaviest trials His confidence never for a moment forsook Him. He had just complained of the insupportable weight of His mental agonies; yet not so complained, but that He had desired His heavenly Father to glorify His own name, whatever sufferings He might have to endure for that end. For the satisfaction of those who would otherwise have drawn wrong conclusions from those sufferings, the Father answered Him by a voice like thunder, "I have both glorified it, and will glorify it again." Immediately Jesus, with His usual calmness, resumed His discourse respecting the nature and necessity of His approaching death, and confidently predicted:

I. The Issue of His Conflicts.

The world and Satan were His great adversaries: and though by His death they would appear victorious over Him, yet He declared that by His death,

A. The world would be judged.

What we are to understand by "the judgment of this world," we cannot absolutely determine: but we apprehend the import of that expression to be, that His death would be the means of exhibiting in the clearest view, first, the wickedness, and next, the desert of the ungodly world.

Who would have conceived the wickedness of the world to be so great as it really is? Who would have conceived, that, if God Himself should become incarnate, and sojourn upon earth, and cause the light of His perfections to shine around Him, and diffuse innumerable blessings by the unbounded exercise of omnipotence and love, His creatures should rise up against Him, and put Him to death? Who would conceive too, that this should be done, not by ignorant savages, but by the people who had enjoyed the light of revelation, heard His gracious instructions, beheld His bright example, and received the benefit of His miraculous exertions: yea, that it should be done too, not by the inconsiderate vulgar, but by the rulers themselves, and by the priests and ministers of God's sanctuary? This shows what human nature itself is, even under the greatest possible advantages.

But the desert also of the world is manifested to us in the death of Christ: for Christ suffered the penalty due to sin: "to redeem us from the curse of the law, He became a curse." And all the misery that He endured both in body and soul as our surety and substitute, was our deserved portion. He who perishes in sin, must endure it to all eternity. Death, which to Him was the period of His release, will be to the condemned soul the commencement of eternal sorrows.

B. The prince thereof would be cast out.

Satan is called the prince, and the god, of this world, because he exercises a universal government over men who are his willing subjects (Eph. 2:2; 2 Cor. 4:4; 2 Tim. 2:26). That which has given him this power is sin: on account of sin, God has delivered men into his hands as their jailor and executioner. But Jesus Christ has "finished transgression and made an end of sin, and brought in everlasting righteousness"; and has thus rescued from the hands of Satan a countless multitude, who shall be eternal monuments of His electing love and His redeeming power. While yet He hanged on the cross, the Lord Jesus "bruised the serpent's head" (Gen. 3:15); yea, "He spoiled principalities and powers, triumphing over them openly upon the cross" (Col. 2:15). At that moment did "Satan fall from heaven as lightning"; and though he still retains power over the children of disobedience, yet he is forced continually to give up his vassals to the Lord Jesus. Moreover, the time is shortly coming (yea, in the divine purpose it was, as it were, then present), when he shall be bound in chains of everlasting darkness, and be cast into that "lake of fire" which has from the beginning been "prepared for him and for his angels." Next, our Lord predicts,

II. The Triumphs of His Grace.

By being "lifted up from the earth" was meant His crucifixion. The expression refers to the lifting up the brazen serpent in the wilderness, which was a type and emblem of the death of Christ. Compare Numbers 21:8,9 with John 3:14. The evangelist himself tells us that our Lord intended to intimate the peculiar kind of death which He was to suffer: and the people themselves understood Him as speaking of His removal from them by death (vv. 33,34). Nor did His words convey the idea of uncertainty (see NIV translation): the event was fixed in the divine counsels from all eternity; and He spoke of it as certainly to be accomplished.

Here then are two things to be noted:

A. The event predicted.

Christ will "draw all men to Himself"; He is that "Shiloh, to whom the gathering of the people should be"; and we see on the day of Pentecost the commencement of this great and glorious work. Would we understand precisely the import of the expression, there we behold it exemplified in the clearest view. We must not indeed imagine that every individual of mankind will be drawn to Christ; for in every age many have rejected Him: but some of all nations, professions, and characters, shall be drawn to Him; and at last shall be found a multitude that no man can number (Dan. 7:13,14).

B. The manner in which it shall be accomplished.

Men are not drawn to Him like stocks and stones, but in a way consistent with the perfect exercise of their own free will. The power indeed is Christ's; and it is exerted with effect: but it is made effectual—

First, by showing men their need of Him. The eyes of all the wounded Israelites were drawn to the brazen serpent in the wilderness: they felt that they were dying of their wounds; they knew that no human efforts could heal them; and they were assured that a sight of that brazen serpent would effect their cure. This attraction was sufficient: they looked and were healed. Thus the jailor saw his own perishing condition, and asked, "What shall I do to be saved?" and was glad to embrace the Savior proposed to him (Acts 16:30,31).

Next, He draws men by the attractive influences of His grace. Because men know not how the Holy Spirit works upon the souls of men, they are ready to doubt, or even deny, His operations. But who doubts the agency of the wind? Yet no man knows whence it comes, or whither it goes. It is visible in its effects; and therefore its operation is acknowledged, notwithstanding it is involved in the deepest mystery. Why then should the operation of the Holy Spirit be doubted, merely because the mode of His agency is not understood? (John 3:8). Were it possible to question the evidence of our sense, we should deny the virtue of the loadstone, and represent anyone as weak or wicked who should profess to believe it. But we behold its effects; and our incredulity is vanquished. So then must we confess the agency of the thing respecting it. Our Lord has told us that "no man can come unto Him, except the Father draw him" (John 6:44); and the Psalmist affirms that God makes us "willing in the day of His power" (Ps. 110:3). It is sufficient for us to know that He draws us rationally "with the bands of love."

Lastly, He draws men by discovering to them the wonders of His love. Let but a glimpse of His incomprehensible love be seen, and everything in the whole creation will be darkened: just as a view of the meridian sun renders every other object invisible. Paul tells us that "the love of Christ constrained Him." As well might the angels in heaven be averse to serve their God, as the man that has tasted of redeeming love.

In this way then does the grace of Christ prevail; and in this way shall it triumph to the ends of the earth.

Application:
1. Seek to experience the attractions of His grace. Nothing under heaven is so desirable as this.
2. Fear not the counteracting influence of men or devils. Men may oppose you, and vaunt themselves against you: but they are already "judged" by the Word of God; and, if they repent not, they shall be judged by the same at the tribunal of their God.

    Satan too may harass you: but he is a vanquished enemy: yea, he too "is judged" (John 16:11); and though, "as a roaring lion, he seeketh to devour you," you are provided with armor, whereby you may withstand him (Eph. 6:11-13); and you have the promise of God, that "he shall be shortly bruised under your feet" (Rom. 16:20).

CONDENSED FROM CHARLES SIMEON

THE CIRCUMSTANCES SURROUNDING CHRIST'S DEATH

"And He bearing His cross went forth into a place called the place of a skull . . . where they crucified Him" (John 19:17,18).

The evangelists are very particular and minute in detailing every circumstances connected with Christ's death. At present we design to contemplate, more especially, three things: I. The Place. II. The Manner. And, III. The Astonishing Phenomena Accompanying It. Notice then,

I.   The Place of Christ's Death.

"Golgotha," the place of skulls; the remains of malefactors who had suffered littered the spot. In this place we behold,

A.   A striking emblem of the world Christ came to save.

Here were the trophies of death—the ruins of human nature; here were sufficient evidences of man's depravity, ruin, and helplessness. And such was the condition of the world Christ came to redeem—one region of death—one dreary burial-ground—one vast Golgotha. It was sunk in depravity; exposed to peril the most alarming; and, to human contemplation, in a condition of helplessness. In Golgotha, the place of Christ's death, we see,

B.   Jewish malice and unbelief overruled for our welfare.

Jesus came expressly to His own, to His own people, the lost sheep of Israel; but they received Him not; they hated Him, and persecuted Him, and at last put Him to death—and thrust Him outside the gate of their city. Jesus did not then offer Himself upon a Jewish altar, and thus restrict the merit of His blood to one people; but on the elevated mount of Calvary—on the notorious summit of Golgotha, He died as the propitiation for the sins of the world.

C.   We see in it the *extent* and the *efficacy* of Christ's death.

Christ "came not to call the righteous, but sinners to repentance." He lived and died for the very chief of transgressors. His death at Golgotha speaks the language of hope to harlots, publicans, and thieves. And we know that shortly afterwards, the virtue of His blood was savingly experienced by 3,000 Jerusalem sinners.

II.   The Manner of Christ's Death.

"Where they crucified Him." Crucifixion was a Roman punishment, and was only employed in cases of extreme notoriety; the sufferers were generally slaves, who had been guilty of aggravated robberies or murder. This death the blessed Jesus endured.

A.   That it was a most shameful death.

Associated with the vilest and most worthless of our race; exposure of person, etc.; identified with all that was degrading.

B.   It was a death of excruciating agony.

The body stretched upon transverse pieces of wood; most tender parts torn with the rude nails by which they were fastened. The body thus suspended, scorching thirst would burn up the system; fever would be produced; finally, exhaustion, delirium and death.

C.   It was peculiarly lingering in its character.

Often several hours elapsed before death would release the sufferer. Christ hung on the cross six hours, from about nine in the morning until three in the afternoon. What suffering and woe!

III.   Note the Astonishing Phenomena Accompanying Christ's Death.

There was then,

A.   The unnatural darkness.

The sun was darkened; whole land involved in gloom; not by an eclipse, for it was now full moon, and therefore, if at all possible, could not have lasted for more than a few minutes, this for three hours. Now, indeed, was the hour of darkness; when hell expected to triumph; but when, in fact, the domains of perdition were shaken to their foundations. The conflict was tremendous. The sun refused to give its light, or be a spectator of the momentous scene. Christ's soul, too, was now enduring the absence of Jehovah's smile. Hence the bitter, inexplicable cry: "My God, My God," etc.

B.   The rocks rent, and the earth quaked.

Indicating the removal of the old, and the introduction of a new dispensation.

C.   The graves were opened. For Christ was now abolishing death, by overcoming him who had the power of death, the devil.

D.   The veil of the temple removed. Priests dismissed; legal dispensation abrogated; separating wall between Jews and Gentiles thrown down, and the way opened to the holiest of all.

Application: We have in the place and manner of Christ's death,

1.   Exhibited to us God's displeasure against sin, yet His mercy to the sinner.

2.   We perceive the only refuge for the guilty.

3.   The saint's only hope and glory.   —JABEZ BURNS

IT IS FINISHED

"It is finished" (John 19:30).

These words may be considered as including the following:

I.   **The Sufferings of the Savior Were Finished.**

A.   His humiliation was profound: He condescended to take humanity, was distinguished by poverty, had nowhere to lay His head.

B.   His sufferings were intense: He was mocked, suffered the excruciating death of the cross, endured the thunderbolts of divine vengeance.

C.   But the sufferings and humiliation of Christ were now over.

II. **The Prophecies of the Old Testament Were Now Fully Accomplished.**

A.   The prophets had predicted all the remarkable events in the Savior's life: He was to be born of a virgin, at Bethlehem—to be despised and rejected by His countrymen, to bear His sufferings with meekness and resignation, to be numbered with transgressors, not a bone to be broken, to be cut off, but not for Himself.

B.   These prophecies receive their full accomplishment, as appears from the New Testament history.

III. **The Mosaical Dispensation Was Now Forever Abolished.**

A.   This dispensation was only a typical institution.

B.   It was now abolished. Sacrifices were to cease. The veil rent.

C.   The Jews were no longer the exclusive objects of the divine favor—the gospel was to be preached to the Gentiles also.

IV. **The Redemption of the Guilty Was Now Completely Accomplished.**

A.   Man was in a state which required redemption.

B.   The justice and veracity of the divine character demanded a satisfaction for sin.

C.   This satisfaction was rendered by the Savior—to the extent that the law required.

V.   **The Empire of Satan Was Forever Destroyed.**

A.   The world was in bondage to the prince of darkness—led captive by the devil at His will.

B.   This enemy was conquered by the Savior—at His temptation in the wilderness, when He expelled him from those he possessed, and triumphed over him on His cross.   —SIMEON